D0570456

Table of Contents

(Answer Key in Back)

Thank you moms, dads, and caregivers.
Thank you teachers and homeschooling parents.
Special thanks to all the helpful big brothers and sisters.
Ultimate thanks to the student. It's your effort that matters most!

Have questions, suggestions, or ideas for future resources?
Contact us at www.HumbleMath.com

ISBN: 978-1-63578-307-0

Current contact information can be found at:
www.HumbleMath.com   www.LibroStudioLLC.com

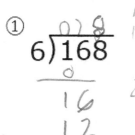

8 ÷ 49   56 ÷ 3,107   640 =

Name: Daemon

Score:

① 6)168

② 9)351

③ 5)440

④ 47)1,176

⑤ 4)368

⑥ 8)232

⑦ 3)291

⑧ 1)993

⑨ 2)1,772

⑩ 5)735

⑪ 9)1,062

⑫ 8)408

⑬ 7)364

⑭ 5)235

⑮ 1)511

⑯ 3)192

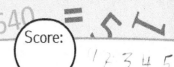

Name: Daemon

Score:

① $\overset{60}{1\overline{)283}}$

② $\overset{49}{3\overline{)690}}$

③ $\overset{70}{8\overline{)480}}$

④ $\overset{42}{4\overline{)168}}$

⑤ $\overset{180}{5\overline{)920}}$

⑥ $\overset{94}{6\overline{)294}}$

⑦ $\overset{14}{7\overline{)98}}$

⑧ $\overset{133}{3\overline{)399}}$

⑨ $8\overline{)864}$

⑩ $\overset{733}{2\overline{)1,476}}$

⑪ $\overset{544}{3\overline{)1,188}}$

⑫ $6\overline{)510}$

⑬ $\overset{7\ 13}{2\overline{)1,526}}$

⑭ $\overset{110}{4\overline{)572}}$ R130

⑮ $\overset{22}{5\overline{)110}}$

⑯ $\overset{66}{6\overline{)444}}$

© Libro Studio LLC 2019

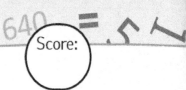

Name: _____

Score:

① $7\overline{)196}$ ② $6\overline{)360}$ ③ $3\overline{)144}$ ④ $5\overline{)205}$

⑤ $8\overline{)72}$ ⑥ $7\overline{)203}$ ⑦ $7\overline{)588}$ ⑧ $2\overline{)1,334}$

⑨ $9\overline{)1,089}$ ⑩ $6\overline{)738}$ ⑪ $4\overline{)396}$ ⑫ $5\overline{)85}$

⑬ $7\overline{)63}$ ⑭ $1\overline{)463}$ ⑮ $2\overline{)200}$ ⑯ $7\overline{)448}$

Day 4
Single Digit Divisors

Name: _____

Score:

① 3)288

② 5)460

③ 6)810

④ 2)24

⑤ 4)188

⑥ 9)495

⑦ 8)144

⑧ 7)266

⑨ 1)12

⑩ 3)1,263

⑪ 6)468

⑫ 2)170

⑬ 9)99

⑭ 4)364

⑮ 3)1,008

⑯ 6)498

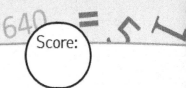

Name: _____

Score:

① $2\overline{)696}$

② $8\overline{)992}$

③ $9\overline{)135}$

④ $6\overline{)1,278}$

⑤ $7\overline{)42}$

⑥ $5\overline{)195}$

⑦ $1\overline{)98}$

⑧ $3\overline{)87}$

⑨ $6\overline{)126}$

⑩ $4\overline{)1,244}$

⑪ $7\overline{)889}$

⑫ $5\overline{)385}$

⑬ $1\overline{)519}$

⑭ $9\overline{)144}$

⑮ $3\overline{)36}$

⑯ $8\overline{)344}$

Name: _____

Score:

① 8)432 ② 2)1,248 ③ 5)195 ④ 3)261

⑤ 4)76 ⑥ 6)390 ⑦ 5)1,980 ⑧ 9)297

⑨ 8)216 ⑩ 3)117 ⑪ 1)27 ⑫ 7)77

⑬ 5)190 ⑭ 9)162 ⑮ 4)272 ⑯ 8)344

Name: _____

Score:

① 4)504

② 6)240

③ 1)339

④ 8)472

⑤ 3)1,941

⑥ 7)1,645

⑦ 2)198

⑧ 5)330

⑨ 9)279

⑩ 6)936

⑪ 3)72

⑫ 5)110

⑬ 2)834

⑭ 7)182

⑮ 8)600

⑯ 3)84

Name: _____

Score:

① 2)‾16‾

② 5)‾440‾

③ 3)‾933‾

④ 9)‾459‾

⑤ 4)‾676‾

⑥ 5)‾230‾

⑦ 9)‾936‾

⑧ 6)‾486‾

⑨ 7)‾1,533‾

⑩ 8)‾1,560‾

⑪ 1)‾24‾

⑫ 4)‾292‾

⑬ 7)‾14‾

⑭ 2)‾1,692‾

⑮ 5)‾275‾

⑯ 8)‾328‾

Name: _____

Score:

① $1)\overline{20}$

② $8)\overline{80}$

③ $3)\overline{1,146}$

④ $5)\overline{1,530}$

⑤ $9)\overline{162}$

⑥ $6)\overline{450}$

⑦ $7)\overline{112}$

⑧ $2)\overline{180}$

⑨ $3)\overline{1,296}$

⑩ $5)\overline{190}$

⑪ $9)\overline{342}$

⑫ $7)\overline{357}$

⑬ $7)\overline{70}$

⑭ $6)\overline{84}$

⑮ $5)\overline{95}$

⑯ $1)\overline{48}$

Name: _____

Score:

① 5)260

② 3)150

③ 7)238

④ 2)630

⑤ 1)718

⑥ 9)576

⑦ 6)336

⑧ 4)900

⑨ 9)432

⑩ 8)400

⑪ 7)378

⑫ 3)1,353

⑬ 2)120

⑭ 7)441

⑮ 9)189

⑯ 4)248

Name: _____

Score:

① 3)225

② 5)405

③ 1)43

④ 9)135

⑤ 3)1,788

⑥ 7)336

⑦ 8)576

⑧ 6)252

⑨ 1)84

⑩ 5)1,605

⑪ 3)45

⑫ 2)1,450

⑬ 5)1,605

⑭ 4)1,452

⑮ 1)12

⑯ 8)624

Name: _____

Score:

① 7)574

② 3)186

③ 9)234

④ 5)145

⑤ 2)956

⑥ 4)844

⑦ 7)427

⑧ 1)24

⑨ 6)498

⑩ 8)1,032

⑪ 2)1,656

⑫ 4)572

⑬ 4)1,332

⑭ 6)336

⑮ 5)55

⑯ 7)287

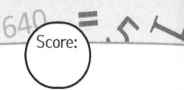

Name: _____

Score:

① 2)28

② 9)126

③ 5)625

④ 8)928

⑤ 6)60

⑥ 7)112

⑦ 2)16

⑧ 5)420

⑨ 3)1,863

⑩ 2)192

⑪ 9)288

⑫ 7)539

⑬ 6)444

⑭ 8)536

⑮ 2)1,122

⑯ 1)14

Name: _____

Score:

① 9)414

② 7)140

③ 9)1,125

④ 2)1,516

⑤ 5)170

⑥ 8)160

⑦ 1)80

⑧ 3)150

⑨ 4)96

⑩ 6)204

⑪ 8)320

⑫ 5)345

⑬ 6)444

⑭ 9)468

⑮ 1)1,456

⑯ 5)140

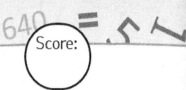

Name: _____

Score:

① $2\overline{)246}$

② $5\overline{)620}$

③ $9\overline{)1,125}$

④ $3\overline{)1,758}$

⑤ $6\overline{)534}$

⑥ $1\overline{)20}$

⑦ $4\overline{)80}$

⑧ $7\overline{)350}$

⑨ $8\overline{)240}$

⑩ $8\overline{)1,344}$

⑪ $5\overline{)450}$

⑫ $1\overline{)960}$

⑬ $2\overline{)10}$

⑭ $5\overline{)25}$

⑮ $8\overline{)40}$

⑯ $6\overline{)288}$

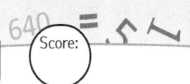

Name: _____

Score:

① 7)924

② 9)711

③ 1)656

④ 2)586

⑤ 3)1,296

⑥ 7)602

⑦ 4)1,568

⑧ 5)1,350

⑨ 9)630

⑩ 8)1,344

⑪ 5)1,890

⑫ 3)960

⑬ 5)1,620

⑭ 7)686

⑮ 9)396

⑯ 2)1,848

Day 17
Single Digit Divisors

Name: _____

Score:

① 4)132

② 1)79

③ 9)1,656

④ 3)693

⑤ 8)432

⑥ 5)1,380

⑦ 2)392

⑧ 6)270

⑨ 7)70

⑩ 2)1,168

⑪ 9)378

⑫ 5)320

⑬ 3)270

⑭ 8)576

⑮ 4)1,152

⑯ 6)924

Name: _____

Score:

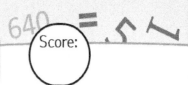

① 8)3,648

② 2)156

③ 5)2,475

④ 7)231

⑤ 3)54

⑥ 4)276

⑦ 6)2,196

⑧ 9)45

⑨ 2)810

⑩ 6)1,584

⑪ 7)42

⑫ 8)64

⑬ 5)1,000

⑭ 1)72

⑮ 7)1,288

⑯ 3)720

Name: _____

① $7\overline{)616}$

② $2\overline{)198}$

③ $9\overline{)495}$

④ $1\overline{)33}$

⑤ $8\overline{)856}$

⑥ $5\overline{)1,070}$

⑦ $6\overline{)366}$

⑧ $9\overline{)918}$

⑨ $9\overline{)81}$

⑩ $3\overline{)264}$

⑪ $9\overline{)414}$

⑫ $8\overline{)448}$

⑬ $6\overline{)1,200}$

⑭ $1\overline{)99}$

⑮ $7\overline{)322}$

⑯ $8\overline{)240}$

Name: _____

Score:

① 8)208

② 4)368

③ 9)3,249

④ 2)78

⑤ 4)20

⑥ 2)428

⑦ 8)7,064

⑧ 6)102

⑨ 5)110

⑩ 1)96

⑪ 9)414

⑫ 8)648

⑬ 8)7,312

⑭ 1)678

⑮ 5)980

⑯ 2)1,548

Name: _____

Score:

① 3)‾2‾3‾

② 5)‾3‾6‾

③ 2)‾3‾

④ 7)‾3‾4‾

⑤ 9)‾5‾6‾

⑥ 5)‾1‾2‾

⑦ 3)‾1‾3‾

⑧ 6)‾2‾3‾

⑨ 4)‾3‾5‾

⑩ 3)‾1‾5‾

⑪ 7)‾3‾7‾

⑫ 4)‾1‾8‾

⑬ 8)‾2‾4‾

⑭ 2)‾1‾8‾

⑮ 5)‾3‾1‾

⑯ 9)‾3‾5‾

Name: _____

Score:

① 8)26 ② 4)13 ③ 6)41 ④ 7)59

⑤ 9)21 ⑥ 8)64 ⑦ 3)20 ⑧ 5)27

⑨ 4)35 ⑩ 7)38 ⑪ 6)15 ⑫ 9)45

⑬ 5)8 ⑭ 8)71 ⑮ 4)36 ⑯ 3)17

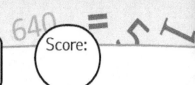

Name: _____

Score:

① 3)22̄

② 9)74̄

③ 4)10̄

④ 3)5̄

⑤ 7)47̄

⑥ 5)15̄

⑦ 6)50̄

⑧ 2)17̄

⑨ 8)34̄

⑩ 3)16̄

⑪ 4)32̄

⑫ 6)34̄

⑬ 4)25̄

⑭ 9)15̄

⑮ 8)39̄

⑯ 5)44̄

Name: _____

Score:

① 6)36

② 4)11

③ 3)4

④ 6)35

⑤ 3)24

⑥ 2)5

⑦ 5)23

⑧ 4)27

⑨ 3)16

⑩ 5)31

⑪ 7)53

⑫ 8)73

⑬ 9)38

⑭ 6)26

⑮ 9)45

⑯ 8)58

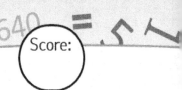

Name: _____

Score:

① 8)45

② 9)36

③ 5)14

④ 4)18

⑤ 9)75

⑥ 4)31

⑦ 7)49

⑧ 6)47

⑨ 8)39

⑩ 3)22

⑪ 5)38

⑫ 2)11

⑬ 6)45

⑭ 2)14

⑮ 6)37

⑯ 4)25

Name: _____

Score:

① 4)1,023

② 3)772

③ 8)521

④ 9)223

⑤ 6)599

⑥ 3)262

⑦ 7)579

⑧ 4)365

⑨ 2)230

⑩ 8)1,160

⑪ 9)1,085

⑫ 5)1,626

⑬ 6)591

⑭ 3)239

⑮ 5)894

⑯ 7)1,427

Name: _____

Score:

① 5)68

② 9)29

③ 7)707

④ 6)8

⑤ 2)1,266

⑥ 4)46

⑦ 3)103

⑧ 8)91

⑨ 3)713

⑩ 6)7,974

⑪ 5)496

⑫ 7)599

⑬ 4)102

⑭ 2)89

⑮ 9)5,679

⑯ 8)1,569

Name: _____

Score:

① 8)552

② 5)72

③ 6)10

④ 9)98

⑤ 3)16

⑥ 4)467

⑦ 2)2,046

⑧ 7)19

⑨ 2)37

⑩ 3)96

⑪ 9)69

⑫ 8)59

⑬ 5)22

⑭ 4)43

⑮ 7)51

⑯ 6)20

Name: _____

Score:

① 4)735

② 6)1,473

③ 7)1,055

④ 3)578

⑤ 2)1,053

⑥ 8)1,170

⑦ 5)555

⑧ 9)107

⑨ 9)3,411

⑩ 8)306

⑪ 4)276

⑫ 3)79

⑬ 5)529

⑭ 7)3,241

⑮ 6)509

⑯ 2)197

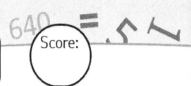

Name: _____

Score:

① $2\overline{)1,831}$ ② $4\overline{)247}$ ③ $6\overline{)158}$ ④ $8\overline{)195}$

⑤ $3\overline{)527}$ ⑥ $5\overline{)149}$ ⑦ $7\overline{)1,579}$ ⑧ $9\overline{)119}$

⑨ $5\overline{)1,435}$ ⑩ $3\overline{)385}$ ⑪ $7\overline{)619}$ ⑫ $2\overline{)514}$

⑬ $4\overline{)1,047}$ ⑭ $6\overline{)3,858}$ ⑮ $8\overline{)147}$ ⑯ $9\overline{)686}$

Day 31
Single Digit With Remainders

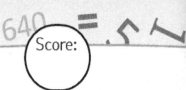

Name: _____

Score:

① 9)159 ② 6)1,806 ③ 3)254 ④ 5)244

⑤ 2)175 ⑥ 7)2,079 ⑦ 8)333 ⑧ 4)131

⑨ 5)374 ⑩ 4)1,289 ⑪ 8)487 ⑫ 3)1,282

⑬ 7)1,658 ⑭ 2)1,071 ⑮ 6)1,088 ⑯ 7)647

Name: _____

Score:

① 3)1,729

② 5)102

③ 7)123

④ 4)847

⑤ 6)875

⑥ 8)746

⑦ 4)13

⑧ 2)787

⑨ 7)448

⑩ 3)23

⑪ 5)84

⑫ 4)275

⑬ 2)74

⑭ 6)539

⑮ 8)307

⑯ 9)235

Name: _____

Score:

① 5)380

② 6)208

③ 8)109

④ 7)218

⑤ 2)147

⑥ 9)383

⑦ 3)363

⑧ 4)395

⑨ 9)269

⑩ 2)142

⑪ 4)166

⑫ 7)685

⑬ 6)429

⑭ 8)971

⑮ 5)880

⑯ 6)269

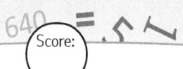

Name: _____

Score:

① 2)1,533 ② 3)138 ③ 7)1,388 ④ 5)309

⑤ 6)1,264 ⑥ 4)309 ⑦ 8)407 ⑧ 9)479

⑨ 5)248 ⑩ 3)150 ⑪ 2)471 ⑫ 6)1,145

⑬ 7)169 ⑭ 4)484 ⑮ 8)539 ⑯ 4)459

Day 35
Single Digit With Remainders

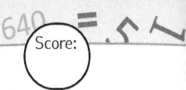

Name: _____

Score:

① 6)402

② 9)418

③ 3)229

④ 2)722

⑤ 5)429

⑥ 7)545

⑦ 4)507

⑧ 2)533

⑨ 8)659

⑩ 7)258

⑪ 4)3,028

⑫ 5)389

⑬ 2)1,729

⑭ 3)1,049

⑮ 6)758

⑯ 5)1,144

Day 36
Single Digit With Remainders

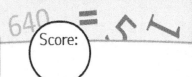

Name: _____

Score:

① 9)179

② 5)468

③ 7)439

④ 3)201

⑤ 4)687

⑥ 6)1,145

⑦ 2)1,261

⑧ 8)379

⑨ 6)874

⑩ 3)1,871

⑪ 2)154

⑫ 7)1,175

⑬ 4)1,083

⑭ 5)863

⑮ 7)1,807

⑯ 9)578

Name: _____

Score:

① 6)195

② 9)278

③ 2)74

④ 4)226

⑤ 3)575

⑥ 5)389

⑦ 7)904

⑧ 6)478

⑨ 8)298

⑩ 7)614

⑪ 5)384

⑫ 4)223

⑬ 9)99

⑭ 2)865

⑮ 4)306

⑯ 7)649

Day 38

Single Digit With Remainders

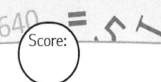

Name: _____

Score:

① 3)112

② 4)343

③ 9)188

④ 5)329

⑤ 2)38

⑥ 6)758

⑦ 8)135

⑧ 7)99

⑨ 5)374

⑩ 8)1,327

⑪ 7)639

⑫ 3)76

⑬ 2)35

⑭ 4)1,300

⑮ 5)344

⑯ 8)648

Day 39

Single Digit With Remainders

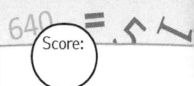

Name: _____

Score:

① $8\overline{)333}$

② $5\overline{)405}$

③ $2\overline{)1,087}$

④ $7\overline{)656}$

⑤ $3\overline{)266}$

⑥ $4\overline{)1,267}$

⑦ $7\overline{)1,698}$

⑧ $9\overline{)1,142}$

⑨ $6\overline{)472}$

⑩ $5\overline{)80}$

⑪ $9\overline{)1,196}$

⑫ $8\overline{)254}$

⑬ $4\overline{)314}$

⑭ $7\overline{)173}$

⑮ $3\overline{)638}$

⑯ $7\overline{)1,053}$

Day 40
Single Digit With Remainders

Name: _____

Score:

① 7)279

② 9)466

③ 5)434

④ 4)895

⑤ 8)564

⑥ 3)188

⑦ 2)166

⑧ 6)124

⑨ 5)395

⑩ 3)298

⑪ 6)130

⑫ 9)323

⑬ 7)97

⑭ 4)255

⑮ 2)278

⑯ 8)727

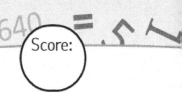

Name: _____

Score:

① 2)393

② 5)218

③ 8)725

④ 3)224

⑤ 7)742

⑥ 9)625

⑦ 6)568

⑧ 9)278

⑨ 2)1,667

⑩ 9)688

⑪ 3)876

⑫ 7)365

⑬ 5)483

⑭ 7)448

⑮ 6)526

⑯ 8)202

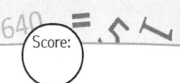

Name: _____

Score:

① 3)1,967

② 8)479

③ 5)597

④ 7)409

⑤ 2)1,524

⑥ 6)496

⑦ 4)238

⑧ 9)277

⑨ 8)264

⑩ 7)465

⑪ 4)499

⑫ 5)429

⑬ 6)968

⑭ 9)779

⑮ 3)266

⑯ 2)267

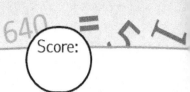

Name: _____

Score:

① 6)330

② 2)365

③ 9)115

④ 3)579

⑤ 7)606

⑥ 8)229

⑦ 5)178

⑧ 6)1,842

⑨ 4)84

⑩ 6)371

⑪ 3)1,247

⑫ 8)451

⑬ 5)169

⑭ 7)860

⑮ 8)298

⑯ 6)136

Name: _____

Score:

① 9)272

② 7)1,798

③ 2)1,315

④ 6)322

⑤ 5)388

⑥ 3)84

⑦ 8)345

⑧ 4)522

⑨ 2)422

⑩ 8)612

⑪ 7)229

⑫ 6)567

⑬ 9)359

⑭ 2)1,237

⑮ 6)373

⑯ 3)227

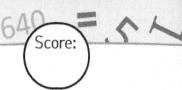

Name: _____

Score:

① 5)103

② 2)114

③ 8)658

④ 9)259

⑤ 7)677

⑥ 6)379

⑦ 4)303

⑧ 3)1,309

⑨ 5)1,059

⑩ 6)87

⑪ 3)326

⑫ 9)145

⑬ 4)395

⑭ 2)479

⑮ 7)629

⑯ 8)904

① 25)‾16,075‾

② 120)‾3,120‾

③ 53)‾1,484‾

④ 15)‾5,805‾

⑤ 40)‾271,800‾

⑥ 326)‾1,630‾

⑦ 717)‾10,038‾

⑧ 95)‾208‾

⑨ 11)‾715‾

Name: _____

Score:

① $29\overline{)17{,}951}$

② $78\overline{)41{,}496}$

③ $315\overline{)28{,}350}$

④ $468\overline{)158{,}652}$

⑤ $83\overline{)3{,}154}$

⑥ $671\overline{)75{,}152}$

⑦ $14\overline{)7{,}924}$

⑧ $55\overline{)35{,}970}$

⑨ $937\overline{)131{,}180}$

Name: _____

Score:

① 36)29,916

② 748)429,352

③ 153)109,089

④ 864)283,392

⑤ 94)57,528

⑥ 576)97,920

⑦ 277)106,645

⑧ 483)15,456

⑨ 63)50,148

Name: _____

Score:

① $49 \overline{)33{,}026}$

② $94 \overline{)79{,}430}$

③ $51 \overline{)47{,}583}$

④ $631 \overline{)42{,}277}$

⑤ $281 \overline{)17{,}703}$

⑥ $376 \overline{)31{,}960}$

⑦ $742 \overline{)60{,}102}$

⑧ $118 \overline{)9{,}204}$

⑨ $858 \overline{)88{,}374}$

Day 50
Multi Digit Divisors

$8 \div 49$ $56 \div 3,107$ 640

Name: _____

Score:

① $63\overline{)56,007}$

② $87\overline{)47,067}$

③ $79\overline{)17,933}$

④ $57\overline{)38,076}$

⑤ $49\overline{)37,436}$

⑥ $99\overline{)84,546}$

⑦ $179\overline{)80,908}$

⑧ $394\overline{)191,878}$

⑨ $219\overline{)17,301}$

© Libro Studio LLC 2019

Name: _____

Score:

① 931)114,513

② 371)29,309

③ 564)6,768

④ 487)18,019

⑤ 723)23,859

⑥ 621)13,041

⑦ 87)15,225

⑧ 13)2,366

⑨ 20)19,980

Name: _____

Score:

① 85)62,560

② 64)33,216

③ 45)29,295

④ 95)43,605

⑤ 618)42,642

⑥ 49)35,280

⑦ 788)329,384

⑧ 823)19,752

⑨ 902)50,512

① $49{\overline{\smash{\big)}\,9{,}212}}$

② $562{\overline{\smash{\big)}\,366{,}424}}$

③ $38{\overline{\smash{\big)}\,27{,}892}}$

④ $410{\overline{\smash{\big)}\,127{,}100}}$

⑤ $544{\overline{\smash{\big)}\,247{,}520}}$

⑥ $349{\overline{\smash{\big)}\,172{,}057}}$

⑦ $47{\overline{\smash{\big)}\,18{,}800}}$

⑧ $53{\overline{\smash{\big)}\,46{,}428}}$

⑨ $38{\overline{\smash{\big)}\,20{,}900}}$

Name: _____

① $666 \overline{)73{,}926}$

② $200 \overline{)124{,}400}$

③ $100 \overline{)73{,}300}$

④ $55 \overline{)10{,}340}$

⑤ $66 \overline{)55{,}440}$

⑥ $77 \overline{)74{,}228}$

⑦ $300 \overline{)284{,}400}$

⑧ $400 \overline{)192{,}400}$

⑨ $500 \overline{)135{,}500}$

Name: _____

Score:

① 86)‾36,636‾

② 240)‾212,640‾

③ 39)‾22,737‾

④ 765)‾75,735‾

⑤ 71)‾2,272‾

⑥ 724)‾100,636‾

⑦ 32)‾30,880‾

⑧ 386)‾145,908‾

⑨ 395)‾137,065‾

Name: _____

Score:

① 425)91,375

② 62)40,858

③ 875)38,500

④ 123)32,472

⑤ 45)40,320

⑥ 678)144,414

⑦ 910)53,690

⑧ 234)39,078

⑨ 567)136,647

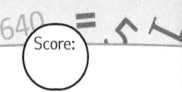

Name: _____

Score:

① 78)52,104

② 24)5,496

③ 384)147,456

④ 12)4,620

⑤ 189)185,976

⑥ 555)42,180

⑦ 49)37,681

⑧ 66)59,400

⑨ 191)35,908

Name: _____

Score:

① $106\overline{)67{,}840}$

② $47\overline{)2{,}209}$

③ $93\overline{)36{,}084}$

④ $475\overline{)83{,}125}$

⑤ $296\overline{)61{,}864}$

⑥ $75\overline{)56{,}775}$

⑦ $542\overline{)47{,}696}$

⑧ $660\overline{)39{,}600}$

⑨ $333\overline{)110{,}889}$

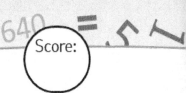

Name: _____

Score:

① 19)10,640

② 29)14,790

③ 59)37,288

④ 81)14,175

⑤ 64)12,096

⑥ 119)107,576

⑦ 542)24,390

⑧ 76)6,080

⑨ 874)39,330

Day 60
Multi Digit Divisors

① $123 \overline{)56,088}$

② $730 \overline{)63,510}$

③ $553 \overline{)196,315}$

④ $15 \overline{)8,175}$

⑤ $91 \overline{)7,189}$

⑥ $16 \overline{)11,904}$

⑦ $225 \overline{)4,500}$

⑧ $442 \overline{)17,680}$

⑨ $159 \overline{)8,745}$

Name: _____

Score:

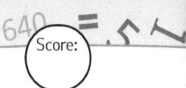

① 27)25,029

② 90)8,730

③ 519)23,355

④ 262)15,458

⑤ 29)7,917

⑥ 161)16,744

⑦ 45)2,025

⑧ 94)4,042

⑨ 254)5,588

Name: _____

Score:

① 435⟌192,705

② 76⟌20,976

③ 10⟌1,100

④ 277⟌26,592

⑤ 29⟌13,021

⑥ 16⟌1,104

⑦ 90⟌4,500

⑧ 111⟌4,329

⑨ 221⟌22,542

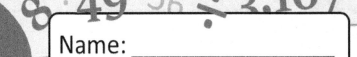

Name: _____

Score:

① $84 \overline{)44{,}352}$

② $325 \overline{)27{,}625}$

③ $62 \overline{)31{,}310}$

④ $127 \overline{)79{,}629}$

⑤ $243 \overline{)10{,}449}$

⑥ $83 \overline{)20{,}169}$

⑦ $59 \overline{)5{,}015}$

⑧ $411 \overline{)143{,}439}$

⑨ $72 \overline{)21{,}024}$

Name: _____

Score:

① $528\overline{)147,840}$

② $15\overline{)8,325}$

③ $750\overline{)56,250}$

④ $13\overline{)16,276}$

⑤ $172\overline{)43,000}$

⑥ $25\overline{)8,300}$

⑦ $115\overline{)9,085}$

⑧ $241\overline{)13,496}$

⑨ $47\overline{)12,925}$

Score:

① $33\overline{)5{,}280}$

② $24\overline{)15{,}552}$

③ $50\overline{)7{,}500}$

④ $313\overline{)6{,}260}$

⑤ $750\overline{)17{,}250}$

⑥ $32\overline{)3{,}232}$

⑦ $77\overline{)7{,}931}$

⑧ $52\overline{)41{,}704}$

⑨ $117\overline{)20{,}475}$

Name: _____

Score:

① 68)51,189

② 83)25,892

③ 75)3,601

④ 20)1,100

⑤ 361)64,980

⑥ 11)7,477

⑦ 666)71,959

⑧ 95)248

⑨ 41)666

Name: _____

Score:

① 885)8,850

② 134)94,069

③ 229)116,569

④ 33)5,245

⑤ 55)34,049

⑥ 66)16,170

⑦ 45)37,896

⑧ 99)52,569

⑨ 77)51,669

Name: _____

Score:

① 781)44,518

② 909)43,639

③ 714)6,426

④ 202)4,446

⑤ 449)38,168

⑥ 37)32,815

⑦ 15)13,969

⑧ 50)23,856

⑨ 62)13,899

Name: _____

Score:

① 60)33,309

② 28)17,975

③ 480)120,480

④ 54)13,935

⑤ 31)14,147

⑥ 102)20,502

⑦ 94)14,967

⑧ 70)55,238

⑨ 841)10,095

Name: _____

Score:

① $556\overline{)71,745}$

② $129\overline{)12,783}$

③ $339\overline{)24,769}$

④ $47\overline{)26,934}$

⑤ $58\overline{)19,898}$

⑥ $69\overline{)31,454}$

⑦ $70\overline{)49,216}$

⑧ $807\overline{)29,024}$

⑨ $908\overline{)46,385}$

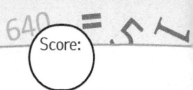

Name: _____

Score:

① $63\overline{)62{,}959}$

② $75\overline{)65{,}711}$

③ $812\overline{)190{,}008}$

④ $307\overline{)155{,}649}$

⑤ $908\overline{)46{,}350}$

⑥ $48\overline{)42{,}624}$

⑦ $50\overline{)35{,}001}$

⑧ $100\overline{)60{,}085}$

⑨ $20\overline{)13{,}996}$

Day 72
Multi Digit With Remainders

Name: _____

Score:

① $490\overline{)29{,}401}$

② $95\overline{)43{,}989}$

③ $82\overline{)25{,}879}$

④ $338\overline{)16{,}224}$

⑤ $210\overline{)53{,}971}$

⑥ $59\overline{)16{,}492}$

⑦ $14\overline{)3{,}926}$

⑧ $749\overline{)50{,}175}$

⑨ $66\overline{)22{,}927}$

Name: _____

Score:

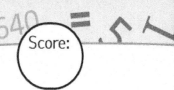

① 38)23,636

② 47)31,270

③ 59)23,246

④ 60)17,735

⑤ 712)57,678

⑥ 890)41,850

⑦ 92)69,143

⑧ 124)52,211

⑨ 214)38,306

Name: _____

Score:

① 253)126,753

② 319)56,473

③ 92)6,385

④ 81)18,977

⑤ 633)450,696

⑥ 19)7,943

⑦ 418)353,298

⑧ 79)11,536

⑨ 546)28,956

Name: _____

Score:

① 17)10,425

② 65)27,179

③ 47)96

④ 98)889

⑤ 223)111,500

⑥ 33)18,843

⑦ 733)58,647

⑧ 55)23,186

⑨ 83)28,169

Day 76
Multi Digit With Remainders

Name: _____

Score:

① 90)73,385

② 11)8,415

③ 21)14,546

④ 31)3,509

⑤ 411)205,500

⑥ 511)475,745

⑦ 61)17,080

⑧ 71)23,172

⑨ 811)90,837

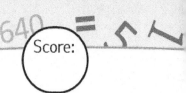

Name: _____

Score:

① $813 \overline{)51{,}223}$

② $773 \overline{)55{,}657}$

③ $611 \overline{)196{,}169}$

④ $53 \overline{)17{,}013}$

⑤ $40 \overline{)5{,}008}$

⑥ $30 \overline{)900}$

⑦ $221 \overline{)80{,}227}$

⑧ $990 \overline{)76{,}235}$

⑨ $131 \overline{)67{,}078}$

Name: _____

Score:

① $746\overline{)21{,}634}$

② $26\overline{)1{,}767}$

③ $315\overline{)40{,}323}$

④ $49\overline{)43{,}262}$

⑤ $86\overline{)68{,}026}$

⑥ $526\overline{)172{,}008}$

⑦ $161\overline{)99{,}984}$

⑧ $66\overline{)7{,}353}$

⑨ $926\overline{)71{,}304}$

Name: _____

Score:

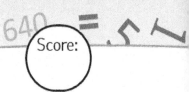

① 68)59,772

② 314)21,038

③ 29)10,027

④ 175)118,831

⑤ 99)37,934

⑥ 88)63,272

⑦ 581)16,856

⑧ 474)16,158

⑨ 74)3,778

Name: _____

Score:

① 515)79,828

② 65)7,999

③ 10)8,116

④ 759)8,349

⑤ 39)11,388

⑥ 271)173,994

⑦ 46)29,458

⑧ 87)2,456

⑨ 941)87,533

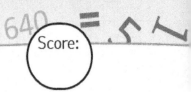

Name: _____

Score:

① 46)12,558

② 773)34,012

③ 51)11,019

④ 37)149,117

⑤ 628)99,255

⑥ 826)324,679

⑦ 176)144,684

⑧ 93)298

⑨ 22)375

Name: _____

Score:

① $361\overline{)148{,}394}$ ② $91\overline{)59{,}293}$ ③ $626\overline{)24{,}467}$

④ $853\overline{)43{,}544}$ ⑤ $24\overline{)15{,}168}$ ⑥ $42\overline{)32{,}977}$

⑦ $533\overline{)28{,}243}$ ⑧ $74\overline{)33{,}337}$ ⑨ $11\overline{)8{,}176}$

Name: _____

Score:

① 24)1,104

② 325)65,003

③ 511)127,239

④ 70)15,126

⑤ 88)26,312

⑥ 946)3,789

⑦ 43)13,536

⑧ 147)10,574

⑨ 68)34,789

Name: _____

Score:

① 129)656

② 73)6,205

③ 443)60,282

④ 62)6,205

⑤ 261)129,978

⑥ 81)1,871

⑦ 329)63,175

⑧ 59)472

⑨ 91)15,116

Name: _____

Score:

① 25)2,083

② 110)4,624

③ 33)2,833

④ 15)5,813

⑤ 70)302,800

⑥ 281)3,630

⑦ 64)10,038

⑧ 58)208

⑨ 16)925

Name: _____

Score:

Directions: *Round the numerator to the nearest thousands place, then divide.*

① $481\overline{)27,438}$

② $639\overline{)83,639}$

③ $85\overline{)7,646}$

④ $372\overline{)6,456}$

⑤ $167\overline{)58,108}$

⑥ $19\overline{)99,465}$

⑦ $27\overline{)14,969}$

⑧ $81\overline{)58,376}$

⑨ $32\overline{)27,809}$

Name: _____

Score:

Directions: *Round the numerator to the nearest thousands place, then divide.*

① $485\overline{)7,850}$

② $65\overline{)74,749}$

③ $269\overline{)356,489}$

④ $37\overline{)7,645}$

⑤ $64\overline{)17,869}$

⑥ $121\overline{)73,170}$

⑦ $45\overline{)11,896}$

⑧ $629\overline{)31,583}$

⑨ $53\overline{)73,099}$

Day 88
Estimation

Directions: *Round the numerator to the nearest thousands place, then divide.*

① 48)5,047

② 14)4,834

③ 76)8,853

④ 15)9,813

⑤ 48)302,800

⑥ 184)5,940

⑦ 103)88,066

⑧ 27)648

⑨ 52)929

Name: _____

Score:

Directions: *Round the numerator to the nearest thousands place, then divide.*

① $75\overline{)33,309}$

② $94\overline{)69,932}$

③ $23\overline{)520,485}$

④ $66\overline{)47,006}$

⑤ $153\overline{)83,597}$

⑥ $94\overline{)30,502}$

⑦ $37\overline{)61,467}$

⑧ $245\overline{)79,638}$

⑨ $377\overline{)25,420}$

Name: _____

Score:

Directions: *Round the numerator to the nearest thousands place, then divide.*

① $36\overline{)100{,}619}$

② $275\overline{)74{,}061}$

③ $117\overline{)380{,}508}$

④ $942\overline{)239{,}619}$

⑤ $49\overline{)74{,}350}$

⑥ $63\overline{)45{,}734}$

⑦ $48\overline{)25{,}701}$

⑧ $83\overline{)95{,}085}$

⑨ $36\overline{)15{,}342}$

Name: _____

Score: ◯

Directions: *Round the numerator to the nearest thousands place, then divide.*

① $64\overline{)93,300}$

② $27\overline{)6,845}$

③ $65\overline{)22,846}$

④ $40\overline{)4,694}$

⑤ $396\overline{)585,500}$

⑥ $511\overline{)308,465}$

⑦ $12\overline{)61,082}$

⑧ $48\overline{)26,172}$

⑨ $773\overline{)89,837}$

Name: _____

Score:

Directions: *Round the numerator to the nearest thousands place, then divide.*

① $36\overline{)19,499}$

② $17\overline{)26,179}$

③ $59\overline{)9,535}$

④ $52\overline{)736}$

⑤ $418\overline{)111,500}$

⑥ $83\overline{)58,843}$

⑦ $933\overline{)63,647}$

⑧ $346\overline{)73,198}$

⑨ $28\overline{)94,169}$

Directions: *Round the numerator to the nearest thousands place, then divide.*

① $56\overline{)55{,}634}$

② $81\overline{)2{,}493}$

③ $375\overline{)89{,}653}$

④ $49\overline{)43{,}262}$

⑤ $86\overline{)68{,}026}$

⑥ $274\overline{)172{,}008}$

⑦ $161\overline{)99{,}984}$

⑧ $66\overline{)7{,}353}$

⑨ $926\overline{)71{,}304}$

Name: _____

Directions: *Round the numerator to the nearest thousands place, then divide.*

① $556\overline{)71{,}745}$ ② $129\overline{)12{,}783}$ ③ $339\overline{)24{,}769}$

④ $47\overline{)26{,}934}$ ⑤ $58\overline{)19{,}898}$ ⑥ $69\overline{)31{,}454}$

⑦ $70\overline{)49{,}216}$ ⑧ $807\overline{)29{,}024}$ ⑨ $908\overline{)46{,}385}$

÷49 56 ÷ 3.107 640 =

Name: _____

Score:

Directions: *Round the numerator to the nearest thousands place, then divide.*

① 732)89,401

② 54)33,489

③ 79)48,879

④ 27)16,224

⑤ 556)14,971

⑥ 812)96,472

⑦ 634)9,915

⑧ 49)58,183

⑨ 36)45,927

Name: _____

Score:

(1) Janet's blog post received 57,890 views this week. How many views is that per day?

(2) There are 279 pieces of pizza for the music students. If there are 93 music students, how many pieces of pizza can each student have?

(3) A store hopes to sell 1800 backpacks during its 30-day sale. How many backpacks would it need to sell each day to meet this goal?

(4) After 22 days of the backpack sale, a total of 1539 backpacks have been sold. Roughly how many backpacks have been sold each day?

Name: _____

Score: _____

(1) A chicken farmer hatches 5,424 chicks and needs to split them up evenly between the farm's eight barns. How many chicks should be put in each barn?

(2) The farm produces about 17,500 eggs each week. The eggs are sold by the dozen. How many dozen is this per week? *(Round your answer to the nearest whole number)*

(3) On average, how many eggs would need to be laid each day for the chickens to produce 17,500 eggs a week?

(4) Each week the 17,500 eggs are loaded onto delivery trucks. Each truck can hold 3000 eggs. How many trucks are needed to deliver these eggs?

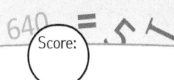
(1) The school buys 2,400 crayons at the beginning of the year. They buy and equal amount of 8 different colors. How many of each color did the school buy?

(2) The 2,400 crayons were delivered to the school in 40 different boxes. How many crayons were in each box?

(3) There are 15 classrooms in the school. The principal wants the 2,400 crayons split up evenly between each class. How many crayons should each classroom get?

(4) before the end of the year the crayons are running out. The principal orders another 540 crayons and distributes them evenly to each of the classrooms. How many crayons each classroom get this time?

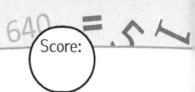

Name: _____

Score:

① Jack is building a city out of blocks. He has made 9 buildings so far and used 3,492 blocks. On average, how many blocks did he use for each of the buildings?

② He wants to build 14 buildings and wants each of them to have the same number of windows. If he has 112 window pieces, how many should each building get?

③ Jack has 56 toy people to put in the buildings. If he divides them evenly between the 14 buildings, how many will each building get?

④ Jack has an equal amount of six different colors of blocks. If he has a total of 3,492 blocks, how many blocks do each of the colors have?

(1) Elizabeth loves to read. Her goal is to read 20,000 pages in one year. How many pages would she need to read each month to make this goal?

(2) Elizabeth thinks that is a lot of pages to read each month, but hopes that the number of pages she would have to read each day will sound more manageable. If she wants to read 20,000 pages in 365 days, how many pages would she need to read each day?

(3) Elizabeth's class hears about her reading goal and decide that they want to make a class goal. They want the class to read 25,000 in one month. There are 28 kids in her class. How many pages will each student need to read to make this goal?

(4) There are 30 days during the month of their goal. How many pages will the whole class need to read each day to complete their goal of 25,000 pages by the end of the month?

Answer Key

Day 1:
1) 28 2) 39 3) 88 4) 168
5) 92 6) 29 7) 97 8) 993
9) 886 10) 147 11) 118 12) 51
13) 52 14) 47 15) 511 16) 64

Day 2:
1) 283 2) 230 3) 60 4) 42
5) 184 6) 49 7) 14 8) 133
9) 108 10) 738 11) 396 12) 85
13) 763 14) 143 15) 22 16) 74

Day 3:
1) 28 2) 60 3) 48 4) 41
5) 9 6) 29 7) 84 8) 667
9) 121 10) 123 11) 99 12) 17
13) 9 14) 463 15) 100 16) 64

Day 4:
1) 96 2) 92 3) 135 4) 12
5) 47 6) 55 7) 18 8) 38
9) 12 10) 421 11) 78 12) 85
13) 11 14) 91 15) 336 16) 83

Day 5:
1) 348 2) 124 3) 15 4) 213
5) 6 6) 39 7) 98 8) 29
9) 21 10) 311 11) 127 12) 77
13) 519 14) 16 15) 12 16) 43

Day 6:
1) 54 2) 624 3) 39 4) 87
5) 19 6) 65 7) 396 8) 33
9) 27 10) 39 11) 27 12) 11
13) 38 14) 18 15) 68 16) 43

Day 7:
1) 126 2) 40 3) 339 4) 59
5) 647 6) 235 7) 99 8) 66
9) 31 10) 156 11) 24 12) 22
13) 417 14) 26 15) 75 16) 28

Day 8:
1) 8 2) 88 3) 311 4) 51
5) 169 6) 46 7) 104 8) 81
9) 219 10) 195 11) 24 12) 73
13) 2 14) 846 15) 55 16) 41

Day 9:
1) 20 2) 10 3) 382 4) 306
5) 18 6) 75 7) 16 8) 90
9) 432 10) 38 11) 38 12) 51
13) 10 14) 14 15) 19 16) 48

Day 10:
1) 52 2) 50 3) 34 4) 315
5) 718 6) 64 7) 56 8) 225
9) 48 10) 50 11) 54 12) 451
13) 60 14) 63 15) 21 16) 62

Day 11:
1) 75 2) 81 3) 43 4) 15
5) 596 6) 48 7) 72 8) 42
9) 84 10) 321 11) 15 12) 725
13) 321 14) 363 15) 12 16) 78

Day 12:
1) 82 2) 62 3) 26 4) 29
5) 478 6) 211 7) 61 8) 24
9) 83 10) 129 11) 828 12) 143
13) 333 14) 56 15) 11 16) 41

Day 13:
1) 14 2) 14 3) 125 4) 116
5) 10 6) 16 7) 8 8) 84
9) 621 10) 96 11) 32 12) 77
13) 74 14) 67 15) 561 16) 14

Day 14:
1) 46 2) 20 3) 125 4) 758
5) 34 6) 20 7) 80 8) 50
9) 24 10) 34 11) 40 12) 69
13) 74 14) 52 15) 1,456 16) 28

Day 15:
1) 123 2) 124 3) 125 4) 586
5) 89 6) 20 7) 20 8) 50
9) 30 10) 168 11) 90 12) 960
13) 5 14) 5 15) 5 16) 48

Day 16:
1) 132 2) 79 3) 656 4) 293
5) 432 6) 86 7) 392 8) 270
9) 70 10) 168 11) 378 12) 320
13) 324 14) 98 15) 44 16) 924

Day 17:
1) 33 2) 79 3) 184 4) 231
5) 54 6) 276 7) 196 8) 45
9) 10 10) 584 11) 42 12) 64
13) 90 14) 72 15) 288 16) 154

Day 18:
1) 456 2) 78 3) 495 4) 33
5) 18 6) 69 7) 366 8) 5
9) 405 10) 264 11) 6 12) 8
13) 200 14) 72 15) 184 16) 240

Day 19:
1) 88 2) 99 3) 55 4) 33
5) 107 6) 214 7) 61 8) 102
9) 9 10) 88 11) 46 12) 56
13) 200 14) 99 15) 46 16) 30

Day 20:
1) 26 2) 92 3) 361 4) 39
5) 5 6) 214 7) 883 8) 17
9) 22 10) 96 11) 46 12) 81
13) 914 14) 678 15) 196 16) 774

Day 21:
1) 7 R 2 2) 7 R 1 3) 1 R 1 4) 4 R 6
5) 6 R 2 6) 2 R 2 7) 4 R 1 8) 3 R 5
9) 8 R 3 10) 5 11) 5 R 2 12) 4 R 2
13) 3 14) 9 15) 6 R 1 16) 3 R 8

Day 22:
1) 3 R 2 2) 3 R 1 3) 6 R 5 4) 8 R 3
5) 2 R 3 6) 8 7) 6 R 2 8) 5 R 2
9) 8 R 3 10) 5 R 3 11) 2 R 3 12) 5
13) 1 R 3 14) 8 R 7 15) 9 16) 5 R 2

Day 23:
1) 7 R 1 2) 8 R 2 3) 2 R 2 4) 1 R 2
5) 6 R 5 6) 3 7) 8 R 2 8) 8 R 1
9) 4 R 2 10) 5 R 1 11) 8 12) 5 R 4
13) 6 R 1 14) 1 R 6 15) 4 R 7 16) 8 R 4

Day 24:
1) 6 2) 2 R 3 3) 1 R 1 4) 5 R 5
5) 8 6) 2 R 1 7) 4 R 3 8) 6 R 3
9) 5 R 1 10) 6 R 1 11) 7 R 4 12) 9 R 1
13) 4 R 2 14) 4 R 2 15) 5 16) 7 R 2

Day 25:
1) 5 R 5 2) 4 3) 2 R 4 4) 4 R 2
5) 8 R 3 6) 7 R 3 7) 7 8) 7 R 5
9) 4 R 7 10) 7 R 1 11) 7 R 3 12) 5 R 1
13) 7 R 3 14) 7 15) 6 R 1 16) 6 R 1

Day 26:
1) 255 R 3 2) 257 R 1 3) 65 R 1 4) 24 R 7
5) 99 R 5 6) 87 R 1 7) 82 R 5 8) 91 R 1
9) 115 10) 145 11) 120 R 5 12) 325 R 1
13) 98 R 3 14) 79 R 2 15) 178 R 4 16) 203 R 6

Day 27:
1) 13 R 3 2) 3 R 2 3) 101 4) 1 R 2
5) 633 6) 11 R 2 7) 34 R 1 8) 11 R 3
9) 237 R 2 10) 1,329 11) 99 R 1 12) 85 R 4
13) 25 R 2 14) 44 R 1 15) 631 16) 196 R 1

Day 28:
1) 69 2) 14 R 2 3) 1 R 4 4) 10 R 8
5) 5 R 1 6) 116 R 3 7) 1,023 8) 2 R 5
9) 18 R 1 10) 32 11) 7 R 6 12) 7 R 3
13) 4 R 2 14) 10 R 3 15) 7 R 2 16) 3 R 2

Day 29:
1) 183 R 3 2) 245 R 3 3) 150 R 5 4) 192 R 2
5) 526 R 1 6) 146 R 2 7) 111 8) 11 R 8
9) 379 10) 38 R 2 11) 69 12) 26 R 1
13) 105 R 4 14) 463 15) 84 R 5 16) 98 R 1

Day 30:
1) 915 R 1 2) 61 R 3 3) 26 R 2 4) 24 R 3
5) 175 R 2 6) 29 R 4 7) 225 R 4 8) 13 R 2
9) 287 10) 128 R 1 11) 88 R 3 12) 257
13) 261 R 3 14) 643 15) 18 R 3 16) 76 R 2

Answer Key

Day 31:
1) 17 R 6 2) 301 3) 84 R 2 4) 48 R 4
5) 87 R 1 6) 297 7) 41 R 5 8) 32 R 3
9) 74 R 4 10) 322 R 1 11) 60 R 7 12) 427 R 1
13) 236 R 6 14) 535 R 1 15) 181 R 2 16) 92 R 3

Day 32:
1) 576 R 1 2) 20 R 2 3) 17 R 4 4) 211 R 3
5) 145 R 5 6) 93 R 2 7) 3 R 1 8) 393 R 1
9) 64 10) 7 R 2 11) 16 R 4 12) 68 R 3
13) 37 14) 89 R 5 15) 38 R 3 16) 26 R 1

Day 33:
1) 76 2) 34 R 4 3) 13 R 5 4) 31 R 1
5) 73 R 1 6) 42 R 5 7) 121 8) 98 R 3
9) 29 R 8 10) 71 11) 41 R 2 12) 97 R 6
13) 71 R 3 14) 121 R 3 15) 176 16) 44 R 5

Day 34:
1) 766 R 1 2) 46 3) 198 R 2 4) 61 R 4
5) 210 R 4 6) 77 R 1 7) 50 R 7 8) 53 R 2
9) 49 R 3 10) 50 11) 235 R 1 12) 190 R 5
13) 24 R 1 14) 121 15) 67 R 3 16) 114 R 3

Day 35:
1) 67 2) 46 R 4 3) 76 R 1 4) 361
5) 85 R 4 6) 77 R 6 7) 126 R 3 8) 266 R 1
9) 82 R 3 10) 36 R 6 11) 757 12) 77 R 4
13) 864 R 1 14) 349 R 2 15) 126 R 2 16) 228 R 4

Day 36:
1) 19 R 8 2) 93 R 3 3) 62 R 5 4) 67
5) 171 R 3 6) 190 R 5 7) 630 R 1 8) 47 R 3
9) 145 R 4 10) 623 R 2 11) 77 12) 167 R 6
13) 270 R 3 14) 172 R 3 15) 258 R 1 16) 64 R 2

Day 37:
1) 32 R 3 2) 30 R 8 3) 37 4) 56 R 2
5) 191 R 2 6) 77 R 4 7) 129 R 1 8) 79 R 4
9) 37 R 2 10) 87 R 5 11) 76 R 4 12) 55 R 3
13) 11 14) 432 R 1 15) 76 R 2 16) 92 R 5

Day 38:
1) 37 R 1 2) 85 R 3 3) 20 R 8 4) 65 R 4
5) 19 6) 126 R 2 7) 16 R 7 8) 14 R 1
9) 74 R 4 10) 165 R 7 11) 91 R 2 12) 25 R 1
13) 17 R 1 14) 325 15) 68 R 4 16) 81

Day 39:
1) 41 R 5 2) 81 3) 543 R 1 4) 93 R 5
5) 88 R 2 6) 316 R 3 7) 242 R 4 8) 126 R 8
9) 78 R 4 10) 16 11) 132 R 8 12) 31 R 6
13) 78 R 2 14) 24 R 5 15) 212 R 2 16) 150 R 3

Day 40:
1) 39 R 6 2) 51 R 7 3) 86 R 4 4) 223 R 3
5) 70 R 4 6) 62 R 2 7) 83 8) 20 R 4
9) 79 10) 99 R 1 11) 21 R 4 12) 35 R 8
13) 13 R 6 14) 63 R 3 15) 139 16) 90 R 7

Day 41:
1) 196 R 1 2) 43 R 3 3) 90 R 5 4) 74 R 2
5) 106 6) 69 R 4 7) 94 R 4 8) 30 R 8
9) 833 R 1 10) 76 R 4 11) 292 12) 52 R 1
13) 96 R 3 14) 64 15) 87 R 4 16) 25 R 2

Day 42:
1) 655 R 2 2) 59 R 7 3) 119 R 2 4) 58 R 3
5) 762 6) 82 R 4 7) 59 R 2 8) 30 R 7
9) 33 10) 66 R 3 11) 124 R 3 12) 85 R 4
13) 161 R 2 14) 86 R 5 15) 88 R 2 16) 133 R 1

Day 43:
1) 55 2) 182 R 1 3) 12 R 7 4) 193
5) 86 R 4 6) 28 R 5 7) 35 R 3 8) 307
9) 21 10) 61 R 5 11) 415 R 2 12) 56 R 3
13) 33 R 4 14) 122 R 6 15) 37 R 2 16) 22 R 4

Day 44:
1) 30 R 2 2) 256 R 6 3) 657 R 1 4) 53 R 4
5) 77 R 3 6) 28 7) 43 R 1 8) 130 R 2
9) 211 10) 76 R 4 11) 32 R 5 12) 94 R 3
13) 39 R 8 14) 618 R 1 15) 62 R 1 16) 75 R 2

Day 45:
1) 20 R 3 2) 57 3) 82 R 2 4) 28 R 7
5) 96 R 5 6) 63 R 1 7) 75 R 3 8) 436 R 1
9) 211 R 4 10) 14 R 3 11) 108 R 2 12) 16 R 1
13) 98 R 3 14) 239 R 1 15) 89 R 6 16) 113

Day 46:
1) 643 2) 26 3) 28
4) 387 5) 6,795 6) 5
7) 14 8) 2 R 18 9) 65

Day 47:
1) 619 2) 532 3) 90
4) 339 5) 38 6) 112
7) 566 8) 654 9) 140

Day 48:
1) 831 2) 574 3) 713
4) 328 5) 612 6) 170
7) 385 8) 32 9) 796

Day 49:
1) 674 2) 845 3) 933
4) 67 5) 63 6) 85
7) 81 8) 78 9) 103

Day 50:
1) 889 2) 541 3) 227
4) 668 5) 764 6) 854
7) 452 8) 487 9) 79

Day 51:
1) 123 2) 79 3) 12
4) 37 5) 33 6) 21
7) 175 8) 182 9) 999

Day 52:
1) 736 2) 519 3) 651
4) 459 5) 69 6) 720
7) 418 8) 24 9) 56

Day 53:
1) 188 2) 652 3) 734
4) 310 5) 455 6) 493
7) 400 8) 876 9) 550

Day 54:
1) 111 2) 622 3) 733
4) 188 5) 840 6) 964
7) 948 8) 481 9) 271

Day 55:
1) 426 2) 886 3) 583
4) 99 5) 32 6) 139
7) 965 8) 378 9) 347

Day 56:
1) 215 2) 659 3) 44
4) 264 5) 896 6) 213
7) 59 8) 167 9) 241

Day 57:
1) 668 2) 229 3) 384
4) 385 5) 984 6) 76
7) 769 8) 900 9) 188

Day 58:
1) 640 2) 47 3) 388
4) 175 5) 209 6) 757
7) 88 8) 60 9) 333

Day 59:
1) 560 2) 510 3) 632
4) 175 5) 189 6) 904
7) 45 8) 80 9) 45

Day 60:
1) 456 2) 87 3) 355
4) 545 5) 79 6) 744
7) 20 8) 40 9) 55

Day 61:
1) 927 2) 97 3) 45
4) 59 5) 273 6) 104
7) 45 8) 43 9) 22

Day 62:
1) 443 2) 276 3) 110
4) 96 5) 449 6) 69
7) 50 8) 39 9) 102

Day 63:
1) 528 2) 85 3) 505
4) 627 5) 43 6) 243
7) 85 8) 349 9) 292

Answer Key

Day 64:
1) 280 2) 555 3) 75
4) 1,252 5) 250 6) 332
7) 79 8) 56 9) 275

Day 65:
1) 160 2) 648 3) 150
4) 20 5) 23 6) 101
7) 103 8) 802 9) 175

Day 66:
1) 752 R 53 2) 311 R 79 3) 48 R 1
4) 55 5) 180 6) 679 R 8
7) 108 R 31 8) 2 R 58 9) 16 R 10

Day 67:
1) 10 2) 702 R 1 3) 509 R 8
4) 158 R 31 5) 619 R 4 6) 245
7) 842 R 6 8) 531 9) 671 R 2

Day 68:
1) 57 R 1 2) 48 R 7 3) 9
4) 22 R 2 5) 85 R 3 6) 886 R 33
7) 931 R 4 8) 477 R 6 9) 224 R 11

Day 69:
1) 555 R 9 2) 641 R 27 3) 251
4) 258 R 3 5) 456 R 11 6) 201
7) 159 R 21 8) 789 R 8 9) 12 R 3

Day 70:
1) 129 R 21 2) 99 R 12 3) 73 R 22
4) 573 R 3 5) 343 R 4 6) 455 R 59
7) 703 R 6 8) 35 R 779 9) 51 R 77

Day 71:
1) 999 R 22 2) 876 R 11 3) 234
4) 507 5) 51 R 42 6) 888
7) 700 R 1 8) 600 R 85 9) 699 R 16

Day 72:
1) 60 R 1 2) 463 R 4 3) 315 R 49
4) 48 5) 257 R 1 6) 279 R 31
7) 280 R 6 8) 66 R 741 9) 347 R 25

Day 73:
1) 622 2) 665 R 15 3) 394
4) 295 R 35 5) 81 R 6 6) 47 R 20
7) 751 R 51 8) 421 R 7 9) 179

Day 74:
1) 501 2) 177 R 10 3) 69 R 37
4) 234 R 23 5) 712 6) 418 R 1
7) 845 R 88 8) 146 R 2 9) 53 R 18

Day 75:
1) 613 R 4 2) 418 R 9 3) 2 R 2
4) 9 R 7 5) 500 6) 571
7) 80 R 7 8) 421 R 31 9) 339 R 32

Day 76:
1) 815 R 35 2) 765 3) 692 R 14
4) 113 R 6 5) 500 6) 931 R 4
7) 280 8) 326 R 26 9) 112 R 5

Day 77:
1) 63 R 4 2) 72 R 1 3) 321 R 38
4) 321 5) 125 R 8 6) 30
7) 363 R 4 8) 77 R 5 9) 512 R 6

Day 78:
1) 29 2) 67 R 25 3) 128 R 3
4) 882 R 44 5) 791 6) 327 R 6
7) 621 R 3 8) 111 R 27 9) 77 R 2

Day 79:
1) 879 2) 67 3) 345 R 22
4) 679 R 6 5) 383 R 17 6) 719
7) 29 R 7 8) 34 R 42 9) 51 R 4

Day 80:
1) 155 R 3 2) 123 R 4 3) 811 R 6
4) 11 5) 292 6) 642 R 12
7) 640 R 18 8) 28 R 20 9) 93 R 20

Day 81:
1) 273 2) 44 3) 216 R 3
4) 4,030 R 7 5) 158 R 31 6) 393 R 61
7) 822 R 12 8) 3 R 19 9) 17 R 1

Day 82:
1) 411 R 23 2) 651 R 52 3) 39 R 53
4) 51 R 41 5) 632 6) 785 R 7
7) 52 R 527 8) 450 R 37 9) 743 R 3

Day 83:
1) 46 2) 200 R3 3) 249
4) 216 R 6 5) 299 6) 4 R 5
7) 314 R 34 8) 71 R 137 9) 511 R 41

Day 84:
1) 5 R 11 2) 85 3) 136 R 34
4) 100 R 5 5) 498 6) 23 R 8
7) 192 R 7 8) 8 9) 166 R 10

Day 85:
1) 83 R 8 2) 42 R 4 3) 85 R 28
4) 387 R 8 5) 4,325 R 50 6) 12 R 258
7) 156 R 54 8) 3 R 34 9) 57 R 13

Day 86:
1) 56 R 64 2) 131 R 291 3) 94 R 10
4) 16 R 48 5) 347 R 51 6) 5,210 R 10
7) 555 R 15 8) 716 R 4 9) 875

Day 87:
1) 16 R 240 2) 1,153 R 55 3) 1,323 R 113
4) 216 R 8 5) 281 R 16 6) 603 R 37
7) 266 R 30 8) 50 R 550 9) 1,377 R 19

Day 88:
1) 104 R 8 2) 357 R 2 3) 118 R 32
4) 666 R 10 5) 6,312 R 24 6) 32 R 112
7) 854 R 38 8) 37 R 1 9) 19 R 12

Day 89:
1) 440 2) 744 R 64 3) 26,608 R16
4) 712 R 8 5) 549 R 3 6) 329 R 74
7) 1648 R 24 8) 326 R 130 9) 66 R 118

Day 90:
1) 2,805 R 20 2) 269 R 25 3) 3,256 R 48
4) 254 R 732 5) 1,510 R 10 6) 730 R 10
7) 541 R 32 8) 1,144 R 48 9) 416 R 24

Day 91:
1) 1,453 R 8 2) 259 R 7 3) 353 R 55
4) 125 5) 1,479 R 316 6) 602 R 378
7) 5,083 R 4 8) 541 R 32 9) 116 R 332

Day 92:
1) 527 R 28 2) 1,529 R 7 3) 169 R 29
4) 19 R 12 5) 267 R 394 6) 710 R 70
7) 68 R 556 8) 210 R 340 9) 3,357 R 4

Day 93:
1) 1,000 2) 24 R 56 3) 240
4) 877 R 27 5) 790 R 60 6) 627 R 202
7) 621 R 19 8) 106 R 4 9) 76 R 624

Day 94:
1) 129 R 276 2) 100 R 100 3) 73 R 253
4) 574 R 22 5) 344 R 48 6) 449 R 19
7) 700 8) 35 R 755 9) 50 R 600

Day 95:
1) 121 R 428 2) 611 R 6 3) 620 R 20
4) 592 R 16 5) 26 R 544 6) 118 R 184
7) 15 R 490 8) 1,183 R 33 9) 1,277 R 28

Day 96:
1) 8,270 2) 3 3) 60 4) 69 R 21

Day 97:
1) 678 2) 1,458 R 4 3) 2500 4) 5 R 2,500

Day 98:
1) 300 2) 60 3) 160 4) 36

Day 99:
1) 388 2) 8 3) 4 4) 582

Day 100:
1) 1,666 R 8 2) 54 R 290 3) 892 R 24
4) 833 R 10

Made in the USA
Monee, IL
17 June 2021